MW01059324

The Aquinas Lecture, 1973

THE PROBLEM
OF THE CRITERION

Under the auspices of the
Wisconsin-Alpha Chapter of Phi Sigma Tau

By

RODERICK M. CHISHOLM, Ph.D.

MARQUETTE UNIVERSITY PRESS
MILWAUKEE
1973

Library of Congress Catalog Card Number 73-75504

© Copyright 1973
Marquette University

ISBN 0-87462-138-0

PRINTED
IN
U. S. A.

Prefatory

The Wisconsin-Alpha-Chapter of · Phi Sigma Tau, the National Honor Society for Philosophy at Marquette University, each year invites a scholar to deliver a lecture in honor of St. Thomas Aquinas, whose feastday was formerly March 7. The lectures are customarily given on a Sunday in March. The 1973 Aquinas Lecture *The Problem of the Criterion* was delivered on March 11 in Todd Wehr Chemistry by Professor Roderick Milton Chisholm, Andrew W. Mellon Professor in the Humanities, Brown University.

Professor Roderick M. Chisholm was born in North Attleboro, Mass. in 1916. He earned his A.B. at Brown University in 1938, his M.A. in 1940 and his Ph.D. in 1942 at Harvard University. In 1972 he received an honorary degree from the University of Gratz in Austria.

Professor Chisholm began his teaching career in 1946 at the Barnes Foundation. The next year he was assistant professor at the University of Pennsylvania and in 1947 he returned to Brown University as associate professor. He was chairman of the philosophy department from 1951 to 1954 and became a full professor in 1953. He has been a visiting professor at Harvard, Princeton, the University of California at Santa Barbara, the University of Calgary, the University of Illinois, the University of Chicago, and the University of Massachusetts. Professor Chisholm is a consulting editor of *The American Philosophical Quarterly* and of *Philosophy and Phenomenological Research*. He is a former vice president of the Eastern Division of the American Philosophical Association and has been a member of the executive committee of the Association for Symbolic Logic and of the American Philosophical Association. This year he is president of the Metaphysical Society of America and has been elected one of the five permanent American delegates to the Institut International de Philosophie.

Professor Chisholm is noted for his versatility as philosopher, writer, translator. The major thrust of his study, however, has been towards human knowledge in both its logical and its epistemological aspects. He is co-editor of the complete works of Alexius Meinong and he has translated two books of Franz Brentano. The first semester of this year he was doing research at the University of Salzburg.

The publications of Professor Chisholm include *Perceiving: A Philosophical Study*, Ithaca: Cornell University Press, 1957; *Realism and the Background of Phenomenology*, New York: Free Press, 1961; *Philosophy*, Englewood Cliffs: Prentice-Hall, Inc., 1964; *Theory of Knowledge*, Englewood Cliffs: Prentice-Hall, Inc., 1966; and many noteworthy articles in nearly all major philosophical journals. To these publications Phi Sigma Tau is pleased to add: *The Problem of the Criterion.*

The Problem
of the Criterion

1.

"The problem of the criterion" seems to me to be one of the most important and one of the most difficult of all the problems of philosophy. I am tempted to say that one has not begun to philosophise until one has faced this problem and has recognized how unappealing, in the end, each of the possible solutions is. I have chosen this problem as my topic for the Aquinas Lecture because what first set me to thinking about it (and I remain obsessed by it) were two treaties of twentieth century scholastic philosophy. I refer first to P. Coffey's two volume work, *Epistemology or the Theory of Knowledge,* published in 1917.[1] This led me in turn to the treatises of Coffey's great teacher, Cardinal

---

1. Published in London in 1917 by Longmans, Green and Co.

D. J. Mercier: *Critériologie générale ou théorie générale de la certitude.*[2]

Mercier and, following him, Coffey set the problem correctly, I think, and have seen what is necessary for its solution. But I shall not discuss their views in detail. I shall formulate the problem; then note what, according to Mercier, is necessary if we are to solve the problem; then sketch my own solution; and, finally, note the limitations of my approach to the problem.

2.

What is the problem, then? It is the ancient problem of "the diallelus"—the problem of "the wheel" or "the vicious circle." It was put very neatly by Montaigne in his *Essays.* So let us begin by paraphrasing his formulation of the puzzle.

2. The eighth edition of this work was published in 1923 in Louvain by the Institut Supérieur de Philosophie, and in Paris by Félix Alcan. The first edition was published in 1884. It has been translated into Spanish, Polish, Portuguese and perhaps still other languages, but unfortunately not yet into English.

To know whether things really are as they seem to be, we must have a procedure for distinguishing appearances that are true from appearances that are false. But to know whether our procedure is a good procedure, we have to know whether it really *succeeds* in distinguishing appearances that are true from appearances that are false. And we cannot know whether it does really succeed unless we already know which appearances are *true* and which ones are *false*. And so we are caught in a circle.[3]

---

3. The quotation is a paraphrase. What Montaigne wrote was: "Pour juger des apparences que nous recevons des subjects, il nous faudroit un instrument judicatoire; pour verifier cet instrument, il nous y faut de la demonstration; pour verifier la demonstration, un instrument: nous voylà au rouet. Puisque les sens ne peuvent arrester notre dispute, éstans pleins eux-mesmes d'incertitude, il faut que se soit la raison; aucune raison s'establira sans une autre raison: nous voylà à reculons jusques à l'infiny." The passage appears in Book II, Chapter 12 ("An Apologie of Raymond Sebond"); it may be found on page 544 of the Modern Library edition of *The Essays of Montaigne*.

Let us try to see how one gets into a situation of this sort.

The puzzles begin to form when you ask yourself, "What can I really know about the world?" We all are acquainted with people who think they know a lot more than in fact they do know. I'm thinking of fanatics, bigots, mystics, various types of dogmatists. And we have all heard of people who claim at least to know a lot less than what in fact they do know. I'm thinking of those people who call themselves "sceptics" and who like to say that people cannot know what the world is really like. People tend to become sceptics, temporarily, after reading books on popular science: the authors tell us we cannot know what things are like really (but they make use of a vast amount of knowledge, or a vast amount of what is claimed to be knowledge, in order to support this sceptical conclusion). And as we know, people tend to become dogmatists, temporarily, as a result of the effects of alcohol, or drugs, or religious and emotional experiences. Then they claim to have an inside view of the world and they think they have a deep kind of knowledge giving them a key to the entire workings of the universe.

If you have a healthy common sense, you will feel that there is something wrong with both of these extremes and that the truth is somewhere in the middle: we can know far more than the sceptic says we can know and far less than the dogmatist or the mystic says that he can know. But how are we to decide these things?

3.

How do we decide, in any particular case, whether we have a genuine item of knowledge? Most of us are ready to confess that our beliefs far transcend what we really know. There are things we believe that we don't in fact know. And we can say of many of these things that we know that we don't know them. I believe that Mr. Jones is honest, say, but I don't know it, and I know that I don't know it. There are other things that we don't know, but they are such that we don't know that we don't know them. Last week, say, I thought

I knew that Mr. Smith was honest, but he
turned out to be a thief. I didn't know that
he was a thief, and, moreover, I didn't
know that I didn't know that he was a
thief; I thought I knew that he was honest.
And so the problem is: How are we to distinguish the real cases of knowledge from
what only seem to be cases of knowledge?
Or, as I put it before, how are we to decide
in any particular case whether we have
genuine items of knowledge?

What would be a satisfactory solution to
our problem? Let me quote in detail what
Cardinal Mercier says:

> *If* there is any knowledge which
> bears the mark of truth, if the in-
> tellect does have a way of distin-
> guishing the true and the false, in
> short, *if* there *is* a criterion of truth,
> then this criterion should satisfy
> three conditions: it should be *inter-
> nal*, *objective*, and *immediate*.
>
> It should be *internal*. No reason
> or rule of truth that is provided by
> an *external authority* can serve as
> an ultimate criterion. For the re-
> flective doubts that are essential to

criteriology can and should be applied to this authority itself. The mind cannot attain to certainty until it has found *within itself* a sufficient reason for adhering to the testimony of such an authority.

The criterion should be *objective*. The ultimate reason for believing cannot be a merely *subjective* state of the thinking subject. A man is aware that he can reflect upon his psychological states in order to control them. Knowing that he has this ability, he does not, so long as he has not made use of it, have the right to be sure. The ultimate ground of certitude cannot consist in a subjective feeling. It can be found only in that which, objectively, produces this feeling and is adequate to reason.

Finally, the criterion must be *immediate*. To be sure, a certain conviction may rest upon many different reasons some of which are subordinate to others. But if we are to avoid an infinite regress, then we must find a ground of assent that presupposes no other. We must find an *immediate* criterion of certitude.

Is there a criterion of truth that satisfies these three conditions? If so, what is it?[4]

4.

To see how perplexing our problem is, let us consider a figure that Descartes had suggested and that Coffey takes up in his dealings with the problem of the criterion.[5] Descartes' figure comes to this.

Let us suppose that you have a pile of apples and you want to sort out the good ones from the bad ones. You want to put the good ones in a pile by themselves and throw the bad ones away. This is a useful thing to do, obviously, because the bad apples tend to infect the good ones and then the good ones become bad, too. Descartes thought our beliefs were like this. The bad ones tend to infect the good ones, so we should look them over very carefully, throw out the bad ones if we can, and then—or so Descartes hoped—we would

---

4. *Op. cit.*, eighth edition, p. 234.
5. See the reply to the VIIth set of Objections and Coffey, *op. cit.*, Vol. I, p. 127.

be left with just a stock of good beliefs on which we could rely completely. But how are we to do the sorting? If we are to sort out the good ones from the bad ones, then, of course, we must have a way of recognizing the good ones. Or at least we must have a way of recognizing the bad ones. And—again, of course—you and I do have a way of recognizing good apples and also of recognizing bad ones. The good ones have their own special feel, look, and taste, and so do the bad ones.

But when we turn from apples to beliefs, the matter is quite different. In the case of the apples, we have a method—a criterion—for distinguishing the good ones from the bad ones. But in the case of the beliefs, we do not have a method or a criterion for distinguishing the good ones from the bad ones. Or, at least, we don't have one yet. The question we started with was: How *are* we to tell the good ones from the bad ones? In other words, we were asking: What is the proper method for deciding which are the good beliefs and which are the bad ones—which beliefs are genuine cases of knowledge and which beliefs are not?

And now, you see, we are on the wheel. First, we want to find out which are the good beliefs and which are the bad ones. To find this out we have to have some way —some method—of deciding which are the good ones and which are the bad ones. But there are good and bad methods—good and bad ways—of sorting out the good beliefs from the bad ones. And so we now have a new problem: How are we to decide which are the good methods and which are the bad ones?

If we could fix on a good method for distinguishing between good and bad methods, we might be all set. But this, of course, just moves the problem to a different level. How are we to distinguish between a good method for choosing good methods and a bad method for choosing good methods? If we continue in this way, of course, we are led to an infinite regress and we will never have the answer to our original question.

What do we do in fact? We do know

that there are fairly reliable ways of sorting out good beliefs from bad ones. Most
people will tell you, for example, that if
you follow the procedures of science and
common sense—if you tend carefully to
your observations and if you make use of
the canons of logic, induction, and the
theory of probability—you will be following the best possible procedure for making
sure that you will have more good beliefs
than bad ones. This is doubtless true. But
how do we know that it is? How do we
know that the procedures of science, reason, and common sense are the best methods that we have?

If we do know this, it is because we
know that these procedures work. It is
because we know that these procedures
do in fact enable us to distinguish the good
beliefs from the bad ones. We say: "See—
these methods turn out good beliefs." But
how do we know that they do? It can only
be that we already know how to tell the
difference between the good beliefs and
the bad ones.

And now you can see where the sceptic

comes in. He'll say this: "You said you wanted to sort out the good beliefs from the bad ones. Then to do this, you apply the canons of science, common sense, and reason. And now, in answer to the question, 'How do you know that that's the right way to do it?', you say 'Why, I can see that the ones it picks out are the good ones and the ones it leaves behind are the bad ones.' But if you can *see* which ones are the good ones and which ones are the bad ones, why do you think you need a general method for sorting them out?"

5.

We can formulate some of the philosophical issues that are involved here by distinguishing two pairs of questions. These are:

(A) "*What* do we know? What is the *extent* of our knowledge?"

(B) "How are we to decide *whether* we know? What are the *criteria* of knowledge?"

If you happen to know the answers to the first of these pairs of questions, you may have some hope of being able to answer the second. Thus, if you happen to know which are the good apples and which are the bad ones, then maybe you could explain to some other person how he could go about deciding whether or not he has a good apple or a bad one. But if you don't know the answer to the first of these pairs of questions—if you don't know what things you know or how far your knowledge extends—it is difficult to see how you could possibly figure out an answer to the second.

On the other hand, *if*, somehow, you already know the answers to the second of these pairs of questions, then you may have some hope of being able to answer the first. Thus, if you happen to have a good set of directions for telling whether apples are good or bad, then maybe you can go about finding a good one—assuming, of course, that there are some good apples to be found. But if you don't know the answer to the second of these pairs of questions—if you don't know how to go about deciding whether or not you know, if you don't know what the criteria of knowing are—it is difficult to see how you could possibly figure out an answer to the first.

And so we can formulate the position of *the sceptic* on these matters. He will say: "You cannot answer question A until you have answered question B. And you cannot answer question B until you have answered question A. Therefore you cannot answer either question. You cannot know what, if anything, you know, and there is no possible way for you to decide in any particular case." Is there any reply to this?

6.

Broadly speaking, there are at least two other possible views. So we may choose among three possibilities.

There are people — philosophers — who think that they do have an answer to B and that, given their answer to B, they can then figure out their answer to A. And there are other people—other philosophers

—who have it the other way around: they think that they have an answer to A and that, given their answer to A, they can then figure out the answer to B.

There don't seem to be any generally accepted names for these two different philosophical positions. (Perhaps this is just as well. There are more than enough names, as it is, for possible philosophical views.) I suggest, for the moment, we use the expressions "methodists" and "particularists." By "methodists," I mean, not the followers of John Wesley's version of Christianity, but those who think they have an answer to B, and who then, in terms of it, work out their answer to A. And by "particularists" I mean those who have it the other way around.

7.

Thus John Locke was a methodist—in our present, rather special sense of the term. He was able to arrive—somehow— at an answer to B. He said, in effect: "The way you decide whether or not a belief is a good belief—that is to say, the way you decide whether a belief is likely to be a genuine case of knowledge—is to see whether it is derived from sense experience, to see, for example, whether it bears certain relations to your sensations." Just what these relations to our sensations might be is a matter we may leave open, for present purposes. The point is: Locke felt that if a belief is to be credible, it must bear certain relations to the believer's sensations—but he never told us *how* he happened to arrive at this conclusion. This, of course, is the view that has come to be known as "empiricism." David Hume followed Locke in this empiricism and said that empiricism gives us an effective criterion for distinguishing the good apples from the bad ones. You can take this criterion to the library, he said. Suppose you find a book in which the author makes assertions that do not conform to the empirical criterion. Hume said: "Commit it to the flames: for it can contain nothing but sophistry and illusion."

8.

Empiricism then was a form of what I have called "methodism." The empiricist—like other types of methodist—begins with a criterion and then he uses it to throw out the bad apples. There are two objections, I would say, to empiricism. The first—which applies to every form of methodism (in our present sense of the word)—is that the criterion is very broad and far-reaching and at the same time completely arbitrary. How can one *begin* with a broad generalization? It seems especially odd that the empiricist—who wants to proceed cautiously, step by step, from experience—begins with such a generalization. He leaves us completely in the dark so far as concerns what *reasons* he may have for adopting this particular criterion rather than some other. The second objection applies to empiricism in particular. When we apply the empirical criterion—at least, as it was developed by Hume, as well as by many of those in the nineteenth and twentieth centuries who have called themselves "empiricists"—we seem to throw out, not only the bad apples but the good ones as well, and we are left, in effect, with just a few parings or skins with no meat behind them. Thus Hume virtually conceded that, if you are going to be empiricist, the only matters of fact that you can really know about pertain to the existence of sensations. " 'Tis vain," he said, "To ask whether there be body." He meant you cannot know whether there are any physical things—whether there are trees, or houses, or bodies, much less whether there are atoms or other such microscopic particles. All you can know is that there are and have been certain sensations. You cannot know whether there is any you who experiences those sensations—much less whether there are any other people who experience sensations. And I think, if he had been consistent in his empiricism, he would also have said you cannot really be sure whether there have been any sensations in the past; you can know only that there are certain sensations here and now.

9.

The great Scottish philosopher, Thomas Reid, reflected on all this in the eighteenth century. He was serious about philosophy and man's place in the world. And he finds Hume saying things implying that we can know only of the existence of certain sensations here and now. One can imagine him saying: "Good Lord! What kind of nonsense is this?" What he did say, among other things, was this: "A traveller of good judgment may mistake his way, and be unawares led into a wrong track; and while the road is fair before him, he may go on without suspicion and be followed by others but, when it ends in a coal pit, it requires no great judgment to know that he hath gone wrong, nor perhaps to find out what misled him."[6]

Thus Reid, as I interpret him, was not an empiricist; nor was he, more generally, what I have called a "methodist." He was a "particularist." That is to say, he thought

6. Thomas Reid, *Inquiry into the Human Mind*, Chapter I, Section VIII.

that he had an answer to question A, and in terms of the answer to question A, he then worked out kind of an answer to question B.[7] An even better example of a "particularist" is the great twentieth century English philosopher, G. E. Moore.

Suppose, for a moment, you were tempted to go along with Hume and say "The only thing about the world I can really know is that there are now sensations of a certain sort. There's a sensation of a man, there's the sound of a voice, and there's a feeling of bewilderment or boredom. But that's all I can really know about." What would Reid say? I can imagine him saying something like this: "Well, you can talk that way if you want to. But you know very well that it isn't true. You know that you are there, that

---

7. Unfortunately Cardinal Mercier takes Reid to be what I have called a "methodist." He assumes, incorrectly I think, that Reid defends certain principles (principles that Reid calls principles of "common sense") on the ground that these principles happen to be the deliverance of a faculty called "common sense." See Mercier, *op. cit.*, pp. 179–181.

PROBLEM OF THE CRITERION

you have a body of such and such a sort and that there are other people here, too. And you know about this building and where you were this morning and all kinds of other things as well." G. E. Moore would raise his hand at this point and say: "I know very well this is a hand, and so do you. If you come across some philosophical theory that implies that you and I cannot know that this is a hand, then so much the worse for the theory." I think that Reid and Moore are right, myself, and I'm inclined to think that the "methodists" are wrong.

Going back to our questions A and B, we may summarize the three possible views as follows: there is scepticism (you cannot answer either question without presupposing an answer to the other, and therefore the questions cannot be answered at all); there is "methodism" (you begin with an answer to B); and there is "particularism" (you begin with an answer to A). I suggest that the third possibility is the most reasonable.

10.

I would say—and there are many repu-
table philosophers who would disagree
with me—that, in order to find out whether
you know such a thing as that this is a
hand, you don't have to apply any test or
criterion. Spinoza has it right. "In order
to know," he said, "there is no need to
know that we know, much less to know
that we know that we know."[8]

This is part of the answer, it seems to
me, to the puzzle about the diallelus.
There are many things which, quite obviously, we do know to be true. If I report
to you the things I now see and hear and
feel—or, if you prefer, the things I now
think I see and hear and feel—the chances
are that my report will be correct; I will
be telling you something I know. And so,
too, if you report the things that you think
you now see and hear and feel. To be sure,
there are hallucinations and illusions.

---

8. *On Improvement of the Understanding* in *Chief
Works of Benedict de Spinoza*, Vol. II, trans.
R.H.M. Elwes, rev. ed. (London: George Bell
and Sons, 1898), p. 13.

People often think they see or hear or feel things which in fact they do not see or hear or feel. But from this fact—that our senses do sometimes deceive us—it hardly follows that your senses and mine are deceiving you and me right now. And one may say similar things about what we remember.

Having these good apples before us, we can look them over and formulate certain criteria of goodness. Consider the senses, for example. One important criterion—one epistemological principle—was formulated by St. Augustine. It is more reasonable, he said, to trust the senses than to distrust them. Even though there have been illusions and hallucinations, the wise thing, when everything seems all right, is to accept the testimony of the senses. I say "when everything seems all right." If on a particular occasion there is something about *that* particular occasion which makes you suspect that particular report of the senses, if, say, you seem to remember having been drugged or hypnotized, or brainwashed, then perhaps you should have some doubts about what you think you see, or hear, or feel, or smell. But if there is nothing about this particular occasion to lead you to suspect what the senses report on this particular occasion, then the wise thing is to take such a report at its face value. In short the senses should be regarded as innocent until there is some positive reason, on some particular occasion, for thinking that they are guilty on that particular occasion.

One might say the same thing of memory. If, on any occasion, you think you remember that such-and-such an event occurred, then the wise thing is to assume that that particular event did occur—unless there is something special about this particular occasion that leads you to suspect your memory.

We have then a kind of answer to the puzzle about the diallelus. We start with particular cases of knowledge and then from those we generalize and formulate criteria of goodness—criteria telling us what it is for a belief to be epistemologically respectable. Let us now try to sketch

somewhat more precisely this approach to
the problem of the criterion.

11.

The theory of evidence, like ethics and
the theory of value, presuppose an objective right and wrong. To explicate the
requisite senses of "right" and "wrong,"
we need the concept of *right preference*—
or, more exactly, the concept of one state
of mind being *preferable*, epistemically,
to another. One state of mind may be
better, epistemically, than another. This
concept of epistemic preferability is what
Cardinal Mercier called an *objective* concept. It is one thing to say, objectively, that
one state of mind is *to be preferred* to another. It is quite another thing to say, sub-
jectively, that one state of mind is in fact
preferred to another—that someone or
other happens to prefer the one state of
mind to the other. If a state of mind A is
to be preferred to a state of mind B, if it
is, as I would like to say, intrinsically preferable to B, then anyone who prefers
B to A is *mistaken* in his preference.

Given this concept of epistemic preferability, we can readily explicate the basic concepts of the theory of evidence. We could say, for example, that a proposition *p* is *evident* to a subject S at a given time *t* provided only that believing *p* is then epistemically preferable for S to withholding *p*—where by "withholding *p*" we mean the state of neither accepting *p* nor its negation. It is evident to me, for example, that there are many people here. This means it is epistemically preferable for me to believe that there are many people here than for me neither to believe nor to disbelieve that there are many people here.

Some propositions are not evident but they are beyond reasonable doubt—the proposition, say, that things in the unused room nearby are pretty much as they were when the last person had left it. A proposition is *beyond reasonable doubt,* we could say, if withholding it is *not* preferable to believing it. And so a proposition would be *unreasonable,* or *unacceptable,* if withholding it *is* preferable to believing it.

Again, some propositions are not beyond reasonable doubt but they may be said to have *some presumption in their favor.* I suppose that the proposition that each of us will be alive an hour from now is one that has some presumption in its favor. We could say that a proposition is of this sort provided only that believing the proposition is epistemically preferable to believing its negation.

Moving in the other direction in the epistemic hierarchy, we could say that a proposition is *certain,* absolutely certain, for a given subject at a given time, if that proposition is then evident to that subject and if there is no other proposition which is such that believing that other proposition is then epistemically preferable for him to believing the given proposition. It is certain for me, I would say, that there seem to be many people here and that 7 and 5 are 12. If this is so, then each of the two propositions is evident to me and there are no other propositions which are such that it would be even better, epistemically, if I were to believe those other propositions.

This concept of epistemic preferability can be axiomatised and made the basis of a system of epistemic logic exhibiting the relations among these and other concepts of the theory of evidence.[9] For present purposes, let us simply note how they may be applied in our approach to the problem of the criterion.

12.

Let us begin with the most difficult of the concepts to which we have just referred—that of a proposition being *certain* for a man at a given time. Can we formulate *criteria* of such certainty? I think we can.

Leibniz had said that there are two kinds of immediately evident proposition— the "first truths of fact" and the "first

---

9. The logic of these concepts, though with a somewhat different vocabulary, is set forth in Roderick M. Chisholm and Robert Keim, "A System of Epistemic Logic," *Ratio*, Vol. XV (1973).

truths of reason." Let us consider each of these in turn.

Among the "first truths of fact," for any man at any given time, I would say, are various propositions about his own state of mind at that time—his thinking certain thoughts, his entertaining certain beliefs, his being in a certain sensory or emotional state. These propositions all pertain to certain states of the man which may be said to manifest or present themselves to him at that time. We could use Meinong's term and say that there are certain states which are "self-presenting," where this concept might be marked off in the following way.

A man's being in a certain state is *self-presenting* to him at a given time provided only that (i) he is in that state at that time and (ii) it is necessarily true that if he is in that state at that time then it is evident to him that he is in that state at that time.

The states of mind just referred to are of this character. Wishing, say, that one were on the moon is a state which is such that a man cannot be in that state without it being evident to him that he is in that state. And so, too, for thinking certain thoughts and having certain sensory or emotional experiences. These states present themselves and are, so to speak, marks of their own evidence. They cannot occur unless it is evident that they occur. I think they are properly called the "first truths of fact." Thus St. Thomas could say that "the intellect knows that it possesses the truth by reflecting on itself."[10]

Perceiving external things and remembering are not states that present themselves. But thinking that one perceives (or seeming to perceive) and thinking that one remembers (or seeming to remember) *are* states of mind that present themselves. And in presenting themselves they may, at least under certain favorable conditions, present something else as well.

Coffey quotes Hobbes as saying that

10. *The Disputed Questions on Truth*, Question One, Article 9; tr. by Robert W. Mulligan (Chicago: Henry Regnery Company, 1952).

"the inn of evidence has no sign-board."[11]
I would prefer saying that these self-presenting states are sign-boards—of the inn
of indirect evidence. But these sign-boards
need no further sign-boards in order to be
presented, for they present themselves.

13.

What of the first truths of reason? These
are the propositions that some philosophers
have called "*a priori*" and that Leibniz, following Locke, referred to as "maxims" or
"axioms." These propositions are all necessary and have a further characteristic
which Leibniz described in this way: "You
will find in a hundred places that the
Scholastics have said that these propositions are evident, *ex terminis,* as soon as
the terms are understood, so that they were
persuaded that the force of conviction was
grounded in the nature of the terms, i.e.,
in the connection of their ideas."[12] Thus

---

11. Coffey, *op. cit.*, Vol. I, p. 146. I have been un-
    able to find this quotation in Hobbes.
12. *New Essays concerning Human Understanding,*
    Book IV, Chapter 7, n. 1.

St. Thomas referred to propositions that are "manifest through themselves."[13]

An axiom, one might say, is a necessary proposition which is such that one cannot understand it without thereby knowing that it is true. Since one cannot know a proposition unless it is evident and one believes it, and since one cannot believe a proposition unless one understands it, we might characterize these first truths of reason in the following way:

A proposition is *axiomatic* for a given subject at a given time provided only (i) the proposition is one that is necessarily true and (ii) it is also necessarily true that if the person then believes that proposition the proposition is then evident to him.

We might now characterize the *a priori* somewhat more broadly by saying that a proposition is *a priori* for a given subject at a given time provided that one or the other of these two things is true: either (i) the proposition is one that is axiomatic

---

13. *Exposition of the Posterior Analytics of Aristotle,* Lectio 4, No. 10; tr. by Pierre Conway (Quebec: M. Doyon, 1956).

for that subject at that time, or else (ii) the proposition is one such that it is evident to the man at that time that the proposition is entailed by a set of propositions that are axiomatic for him at that time.

In characterizing the "first truths of fact" and the "first truths of reason," I have used the expression "evident." But I think it is clear that such truths are not only evident but also certain. And they may be said to be *directly,* or *immediately,* evident.

What, then, of the indirectly evident?

14.

I have suggested in rather general terms above what we might say about memory and the senses. These ostensible sources of knowledge are to be treated as innocent until there is positive ground for thinking them guilty. I will not attempt to develop a theory of the indirectly evident at this point. But I will note at least the *kind* of principle to which we might appeal in developing such a theory.

We could *begin* by considering the following two principles, M and P; M referring to memory, and P referring to perception or the senses.

(M) For any subject S, if it is evident to S that he seems to remember that *a* was F, then it is beyond reasonable doubt for S that *a* was F.

(P) For any subject S, if it is evident to S that he thinks he perceives that *a* is F, then it is evident to S that *a* is F.

"He seems to remember" and "he thinks he perceives" here refer to certain self-presenting states which, in the figure I used above, could be said to serve as signboards for the inn of indirect evidence.

But principles M and P, as they stand, are much too latitudinarian. We will find that it is necessary to make qualifications and add more and more conditions. Some of these will refer to the subject's sensory state; some will refer to certain of his other beliefs; and some will refer to the relations of confirmation and mutual support. To set them forth in adequate detail would require a complete epistemology.[14]

So far as our problem of the criterion is concerned, the essential thing to note is this. In formulating such principles we will simply proceed as Aristotle did when he formulated his rules for the syllogism. As "particularists" in our approach to the problem of the criterion, we will fit our rules to the cases—to the apples we know to be good and to the apples we know to be bad. Knowing what we do about ourselves and the world, we have at our disposal certain instances which our rules or principles should countenance, and certain other instances which our rules or principles should rule out or forbid. And, as rational beings, we assume that by investi-

---

14. I have attempted to do this to some extent in *Theory of Knowledge* (Englewood Cliffs, N.J.: Prentice-Hall, Inc., 1966). Revisions and corrections may be found in my essay "On the Nature of Empirical Evidence" in Roderick M. Chisholm and Robert J. Swartz, eds., *Empirical Knowledge* (Englewood Cliffs, N.J.: Prentice-Hall, Inc., 1973).

gating these instances we can formulate criteria which any instance must satisfy if it is to be countenanced and we can formulate other criteria which any instance must satisfy if it is to be ruled out or forbidden.

If we proceed in this way we will have satisfied Cardinal Mercier's criteria for a theory of evidence or, as he called it, a theory of certitude. He said that any criterion, or any adequate set of criteria, should be internal, objective, and immediate. The type of criteria I have referred to are certainly *internal*, in his sense of the term. We have not appealed to any external authority as constituting the ultimate test of evidence. (Thus we haven't appealed to "science" or to "the scientists of our culture circle" as constituting the touchstone of what we know.) I would say that our criteria are *objective*. We have formulated them in terms of the concept of epistemic preferability—where the location "*p* is epistemically preferable to *q* for S" is taken to refer to an objective relation that obtains independently of the actual preferences of any particular subject. The criteria that we formulate, if they are adequate, will be principles that are necessarily true. And they are also *immediate*. Each of them is such that, if it is applicable at any particular time, then the fact that it is then applicable is capable of being directly evident to that particular subject at that particular time.

15.

But in all of this I have presupposed the approach I have called "particularism." The "methodist" and the "sceptic" will tell us that we have started in the wrong place. If now we try to reason with them, then, I am afraid, we will be back on the wheel.

What few philosophers have had the courage to recognize is this: we can deal with the problem only by begging the question. It seems to me that, if we do recognise this fact, as we should, then it is unseemly for us to try to pretend that it isn't so.

One may object: "Doesn't this mean, then, that the sceptic is right after all?" I would answer: "Not at all. His view is only one of the three possibilities and in itself has no more to recommend it than the others do. And in favor of our approach there is the fact that we *do* know many things, after all."

The Aquinas Lectures

Published by the Marquette University Press
Milwaukee, Wisconsin 53233

⌐⌐⌐

St. Thomas and the Life of Learning (1937) by John F. McCormick, S.J., (1874-1943) professor of philosophy, Loyola University.
SBN 87462-101-1

St. Thomas and the Gentiles (1938) by Mortimer J. Adler, Ph.D., director of the Institute of Philosophical Research, San Francisco, Calif.
SBN 87462-102-X

St. Thomas and the Greeks (1939) by Anton C. Pegis, Ph.D., professor of philosophy, Pontifical Institute of Mediaeval Studies, Toronto.
SBN 87462-103-8

The Nature and Functions of Authority (1940) by Yves Simon, Ph.D., (1903-1961) professor of philosophy of social thought, University of Chicago.
SBN 87462-104-6

St. Thomas and Analogy (1941) by Gerald B. Phelan, Ph.D., (1892-1965) professor of philosophy, St. Michael's College, Toronto.
SBN 87462-105-4

St. Thomas and the Problem of Evil (1942) by Jacques Maritain, Ph.D., professor *emeritus* of philosophy, Princeton University.
SBN 87462-106-2

Humanism and Theology (1943) by Werner Jaeger, Ph.D., Litt.D., (1888-1961) University professor, Harvard University. SBN 87462-107-0

The Nature and Origins of Scientism (1944) by John Wellmuth. SBN 87462-108-9

Cicero in the Courtroom of St. Thomas Aquinas (1945) by E. K. Rand, Ph.D., Litt.D., LL.D., (1871-1945) Pope professor of Latin, *emeritus,* Harvard University. SBN 87462-109-7

St. Thomas and Epistemology (1946) by Louis-Marie Regis, O.P., Th.L., Ph.D., director of the Albert the Great Institute of Mediaeval Studies, University of Montreal.
SBN 87462-110-0

St. Thomas and the Greek Moralists (1947, Spring) by Vernon J. Bourke, Ph.D., professor of philosophy, St. Louis University, St. Louis, Missouri. SBN 87462-111-9

History of Philosophy and Philosophical Education (1947, Fall) by Etienne Gilson of the *Académie française,* director of studies and professor of the history of Mediaeval philosophy, Pontifical Institute of Mediaeval Studies, Toronto. SBN 87462-112-7

The Natural Desire for God (1948) by William R. O'Connor, S.T.L., Ph.D., former professor of dogmatic theology, St. Joseph's Seminary, Dunwoodie, N.Y. SBN 87462 113-5

St. Thomas and the World State (1949) by Robert M. Hutchins, former Chancellor of the University of Chicago, president of the Fund for the Republic.   sbn 87462-114-3

Method in Metaphysics (1950) by Robert J. Henle, S.J., Ph.D., academic vice-president, St. Louis University, St. Louis, Missouri.
                                                                                            sbn 87462-115-1

Wisdom and Love in St. Thomas Aquinas (1951) by Étienne Gilson of the *Académie française,* director of studies and professor of the history of Mediaeval philosophy, Pontifical Institute of Mediaeval Studies, Toronto.
                                                                                            sbn 87462-116-X

The Good in Existential Metaphysics (1952) by Elizabeth G. Salmon, Ph.D., professor of philosophy in the graduate school, Fordham University.   sbn 87462-117-8

St. Thomas and the Object of Geometry (1953) by Vincent Edward Smith, Ph.D., director, Philosophy of Science Institute, St. John's University.   sbn 87462-118-6

Realism and Nominalism Revisited (1954) by Henry Veatch, Ph.D., professor and chairman of the department of philosophy, Northwestern University.   sbn 87462-119-4

Imprudence in St. Thomas Aquinas (1955) by Charles J. O'Neil, Ph.D., professor of philosophy, Villanova University.   sbn 87462-120-8

The Truth That Frees (1956) by Gerard Smith, S.J., Ph.D., professor of philosophy, Marquette University. sbn 87462-121-6

St. Thomas and the Future of Metaphysics (1957) by Joseph Owens, C.Ss.R., Ph.D., professor of philosophy, Pontifical Institute of Mediaeval Studies, Toronto. sbn 87462-122-4

Thomas and the Physics of 1958: A Confrontation (1958) by Henry Margenau, Ph.D., Eugene Higgins professor of physics and natural philosophy, Yale University.
sbn 87462-123-2

Metaphysics and Ideology (1959) by Wm. Oliver Martin, Ph.D., professor of philosophy, University of Rhode Island. sbn 87462-124-0

Language, Truth and Poetry (1960) by Victor M. Hamm, Ph.D., professor of English, Marquette University. sbn 87462-125-9

Metaphysics and Historicity (1961) by Emil L. Fackenheim, Ph.D., professor of philosophy, University of Toronto. sbn 87462-126-7

The Lure of Wisdom (1962) by James D. Collins, Ph.D., professor of philosophy, St. Louis University. sbn 87462-127-5

Religion and Art (1963) by Paul Weiss, Ph.D. Sterling professor of philosophy, Yale University. sbn 87462-128-3

St. Thomas and Philosophy (1964) by Anton C. Pegis, Ph.D., professor of philosophy, Pontifical Institute of Mediaeval Studies, Toronto.
SBN 87462-129-1

The University In Process (1965) by John O. Riedl, Ph.D., dean of faculty, Queensboro Community College. SBN 87462-130-5

The Pragmatic Meaning of God (1966) by Robert O. Johann, associate professor of philosophy, Fordham University.
SBN 87462-131-3

Religion and Empiricism (1967) by John E. Smith, Ph.D., professor of philosophy, Yale University. SBN 87462-132-1

The Subject (1968) by Bernard Lonergan, S.J., S.T.D., professor of Dogmatic Theory, Regis College, Ontario and Gregorian University, Rome. SBN 87462-133-X

Beyond Trinity (1969) by Bernard J. Cooke, S.T.D. SBN 87462-134-8

Ideas and Concepts (1970) by Julius R. Weinberg, Ph.D., (1908-1971) Vilas Professor of Philosophy, University of Wisconsin.
SBN 87462-135-6

Reason and Faith Revisited (1971) by Francis H. Parker, Ph.D., head of the philosophy department, Purdue University, Lafayette, Indiana. SBN 87462-136-4

Psyche and Cerebrum (1972) by John N. Findlay, M.A. Oxon., Ph.D., Clark Professor of Moral Philosophy and Metaphysics, Yale University.
ISBN 0-87462-137-2

The Problem of the Criterion (1973) by Roderick M. Chisholm, Ph.D., Andrew W. Mellon Professor in the Humanities, Brown University.
ISBN 0-87462-138-0

Uniform format, cover and binding.